W9-BZO-142

MY GOVERNMENT

STATE GOVERNMENT

by Vincent Alexander

VOTE
FOR
GOVERNOR

Ideas for Parents and Teachers

Pogo Books let children practice reading informational text while introducing them to nonfiction features such as headings, labels, sidebars, maps, and diagrams, as well as a table of contents, glossary, and index.

Carefully leveled text with a strong photo match offers early fluent readers the support they need to succeed.

Before Reading

- "Walk" through the book and point out the various nonfiction features. Ask the student what purpose each feature serves.
- Look at the glossary together. Read and discuss the words.

Read the Book

- Have the child read the book independently.
- Invite him or her to list questions that arise from reading.

After Reading

- Discuss the child's questions. Talk about how he or she might find answers to those questions.
- Prompt the child to think more. Ask: Have you ever visited your state capitol building? Would you like to?

Pogo Books are published by Jump!
5357 Penn Avenue South
Minneapolis, MN 55419
www.jumplibrary.com

Library of Congress Cataloging-in-Publication Data

Names: Alexander, Vincent, author.
Title: State government / by Vincent Alexander.
Description: Minneapolis : Jump!, Inc., 2018.
Series: My government |Includes index.
Audience: Age 7-10.
Identifiers: LCCN 2017056997 (print)
LCCN 2017054676 (ebook) | ISBN 9781624969423
(e-book) | ISBN 9781624969409 (hardcover : alk. paper)
ISBN 9781624969416 (pbk.)
Subjects: LCSH: State governments–United States–Juvenile literature.
Classification: LCC JK2408 (print) | LCC JK2408 .A53
2019 (ebook) | DDC 320.473–dc23
LC record available at https://lccn.loc.gov/2017056997

Editor: Kristine Spanier
Book Designer: Leah Sanders

Photo Credits: Eddie Brady/Getty, cover; Neustockimages/iStock, 1; railway fx/Shutterstock, 3; North Wind Picture Archives/Alamy, 4; Gene Bleile/Shutterstock, 5; ClassicStock/Alamy, 6-7 (painting); Petrov Stanislav/Shutterstock, 6-7 (wall); Michael DeYoung/Design Pics/Getty, 8; Flory/iStock, 9; Andrew Cline/Shutterstock, 10-11; Jim West/Alamy, 12-13; RichLegg/iStock, 14-15; RyanJLane/iStock, 16; Roschetzky Photography/Shutterstock, 17; Hero Images/Shutterstock, 18-19; f11photo/Shutterstock, 20-21; Nagel Photography/Shutterstock, 23.

Printed in the United States of America at Corporate Graphics in North Mankato, Minnesota.

TABLE OF CONTENTS

CHAPTER 1

HOW STATE GOVERNMENTS FORMED

Before 1776, the 13 American **colonies** governed themselves. There was no national government. Why?

LAND CLAIMS
OF THE
THIRTEEN ORIGINAL STATES

There was no nation. That changed after **independence** was declared.

Declaration of Independence

IN CONGRESS. JULY 4. 1776.

The unanimous Declaration of the thirteen united States of America,

The colonies became states. The **federal** government formed. Citizens would follow its **laws**. But states have their own governments, too. Why? Because each one has special issues. State leaders know what they are. They know what laws to make.

TAKE A LOOK!

Some states were formed long ago. Some states are still fairly new. When was your state formed?

Alabama – 1819	Montana – 1889
Alaska – 1959	Nebraska – 1867
Arizona – 1912	Nevada – 1864
Arkansas – 1836	New Hampshire – 1788
California – 1850	New Jersey – 1787
Colorado – 1876	New Mexico – 1912
Connecticut – 1788	New York – 1788
Delaware – 1787	North Carolina – 1789
Florida – 1845	North Dakota – 1889
Georgia – 1788	Ohio – 1803
Hawaii – 1959	Oklahoma – 1907
Idaho – 1890	Oregon – 1859
Illinois – 1818	Pennsylvania – 1787
Indiana – 1816	Rhode Island – 1790
Iowa – 1846	South Carolina – 1788
Kansas – 1861	South Dakota – 1889
Kentucky – 1792	Tennessee – 1796
Louisiana – 1812	Texas – 1845
Maine – 1820	Utah – 1896
Maryland – 1788	Vermont – 1791
Massachusetts – 1788	Virginia – 1788
Michigan – 1837	Washington – 1889
Minnesota – 1858	West Virginia – 1863
Mississippi – 1817	Wisconsin – 1848
Missouri – 1821	Wyoming – 1890

CHAPTER 2

MAKING STATE LAWS

The 50 states are very different. Alaska has the most land. But not many people.

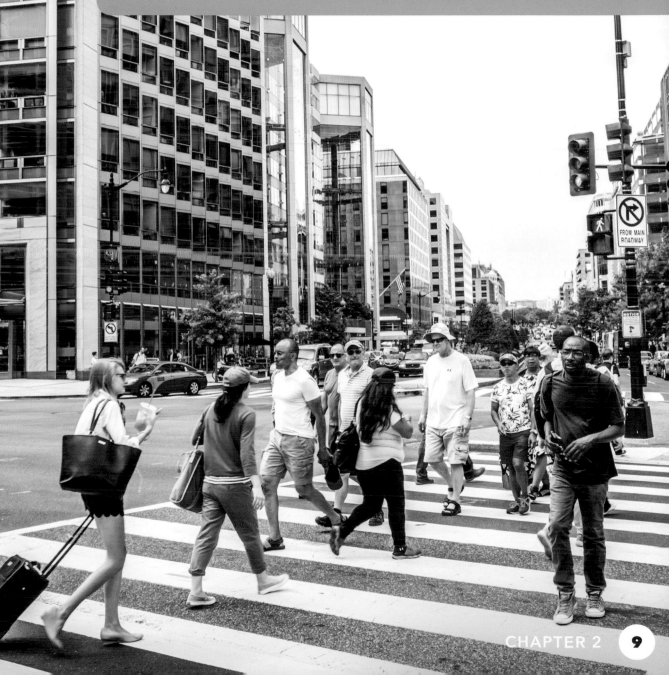

Rhode Island is small. But it is crowded. Land size can determine laws. So can **population**. Who makes the laws?

Just like the federal government, each state has three branches. The **legislative** branch makes laws. About what? Any matter that is not assigned to the federal government. Roads. Hospitals. Schools. Parks. Banking. State resources.

Who is in the legislature? State **representatives** and state **senators**. They serve in addition to their regular jobs.

Michigan House of Representatives

governor

The governor is the leader
of the **executive** branch.
This branch makes sure
that state laws are followed.
The governor also helps
plan the future of the state.

DID YOU KNOW?

In most states, governors
must be at least 30 years
old. Two states have no age
requirements. Which ones? Kansas and
Vermont. Children have run for office!

Every state has a court system. This is the **judicial** branch. It decides if laws have been broken. Did someone commit a crime? A **trial** might take place. Are two people in a disagreement? It could get settled in a court. The state supreme court is the highest court. Higher courts may change the decision of lower courts.

CHAPTER 3

· ·

STATE SERVICES

State governments provide services for the people who live there. Like what? Police protection. **Welfare** for people who need it.

Highway upkeep is another example. **Taxes** help pay for the things states need.

Who pays taxes? Almost all of us! We pay taxes to our state government. We also pay taxes to the federal government.

States receive funds from the federal government, too. Every year the government in each state decides how to spend the money. For example, each state has a **budget** for its parks.

WHAT DO YOU THINK?

Do you like to camp? Your state runs parks with camping areas. What other state services do you use?

Each one of the 50 states is unique. Do you live in a state with a big city? How does it affect your state's laws? State governments know what our needs are. And what challenges we have. The government works for us!

WHAT DO YOU THINK?

What states border your state? How are the laws in your state different from those states?

Chicago, Illinois

ACTIVITIES & TOOLS

START A FOOD DRIVE

States must take care of their citizens. How can you help? Many people need food. You can collect food and deliver it to a food bank.

❶ Visit www.feedingamerica.org to locate a food bank in your area. Have an adult help you call it or read its website to find out what its needs are.

❷ Alert your friends, family, and classmates that you are collecting food for hungry families. Tell them what kinds of foods you are collecting.

❸ Decide how you want to collect food. Friends and family can drop items off at your house. Or you can collect items at school or a sporting event.

❹ Make a flyer about your food drive. Include what kinds of foods you are collecting, where people can drop off their contributions, and which food bank will be receiving the food. Make copies of the flyer.

❺ Hand out the flyers to friends and family. The more people who know about your food drive, the more food you will collect.

❻ Deliver your food contributions to the food bank. And make sure to thank everyone who helped you along the way!

GLOSSARY

budget: A plan for how money will be spent during a period of time.

colonies: Groups of people who leave their country to settle in new areas.

executive: Having to do with the branch of government that carries out the laws of the state.

federal: The central power of the United States.

independence: Freedom from a controlling authority.

judicial: Having to do with the legal system.

laws: Rules made and enforced by a government.

legislative: Having the power to make laws.

population: The total number of people who live in a place.

representatives: People elected to speak for others and make laws.

senators: Members of the Senate who are elected to make laws.

taxes: Money that people and businesses must pay in order to support a government.

trial: The examination of evidence to decide if a charge or claim is true.

welfare: Money or other help given by a government to people who are in need.

INDEX

TO LEARN MORE

Learning more is as easy as 1, 2, 3.

1) Go to www.factsurfer.com

2) Enter "stategovernment" into the search box.

3) Click the "Surf" button to see a list of websites.

With factsurfer, finding more information is just a click away.